BLASTOFF! READERS, AN IMPRINT OF BELLWETHER MEDIA BY FLUTTERBEE

Blastoff! Readers are carefully developed by literacy experts to build reading stamina and move students toward fluency by combining standards-based content with developmentally appropriate text.

LEVELS

Level 1 provides the most support through repetition of high-frequency words, light text, predictable sentence patterns, and strong visual support.

Level 2 offers early readers a bit more challenge through varied sentences, increased text load, and text-supportive special features.

Level 3 advances early-fluent readers toward fluency through increased text load, less reliance on photos, advancing concepts, longer sentences, and more complex special features.

★ **Blastoff! Universe**

Reading Level

Grade
K

Grades
1–3

Grade
4

This edition first published in 2027 by Bellwether Media, Inc.

Text copyright © 2027 by Bellwether Media, Inc. All rights reserved. No part of this publication may be reproduced, stored in any retrieval system, or transmitted in any form or by any means, electronic, mechanical, photocopying, recording, or otherwise, without written permission of the publisher.

BLASTOFF! READERS and associated logos are trademarks and/or registered trademarks of Bellwether Media, Inc. Bellwether Media is a division of FlutterBee Education Group.

For information regarding permission, write to Bellwether Media, Inc., Attention: Permissions Department, 3500 American Blvd W, Suite 150, Bloomington, MN 55431.

Library of Congress Cataloging-in-Publication Data is available at www.loc.gov or upon request from the publisher.

ISBN: 9798898800772 (hardcover)
ISBN: 9798898802011 (ebook)

Editor: Betsy Rathburn Designer: Andrea Schneider

Printed in the United States of America, North Mankato, MN.

Table of Contents

Sick Days

A woman has been sick for many days. Her sickness is hard to treat.

Her doctor calls an infectious disease specialist. This new doctor helps her feel better soon!

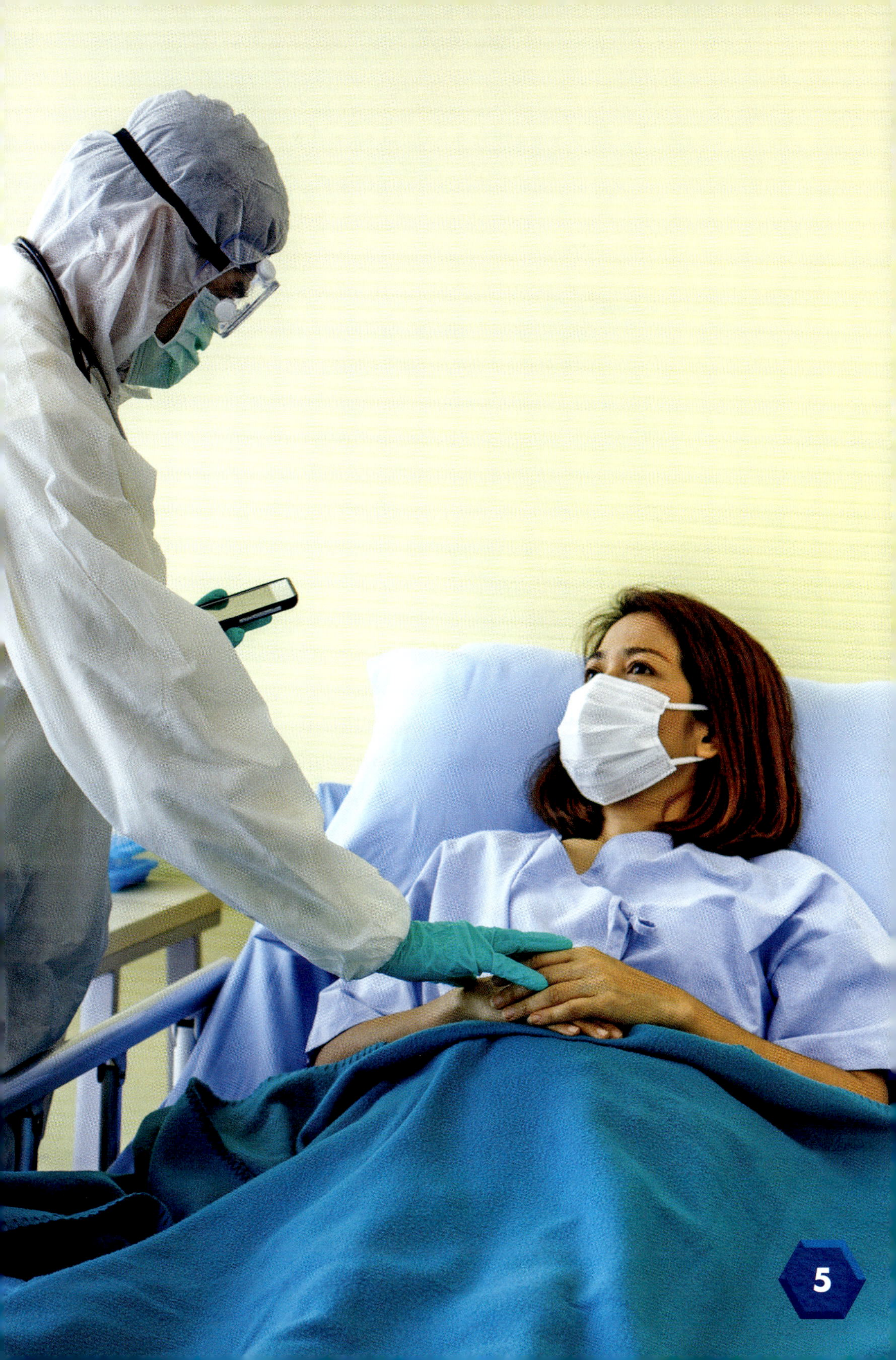

What Is an Infectious Disease Specialist?

Doctors help people who are sick or hurt.

Some **diseases** are hard to treat. Other diseases are **rare**. Infectious disease specialists are doctors. They treat these diseases.

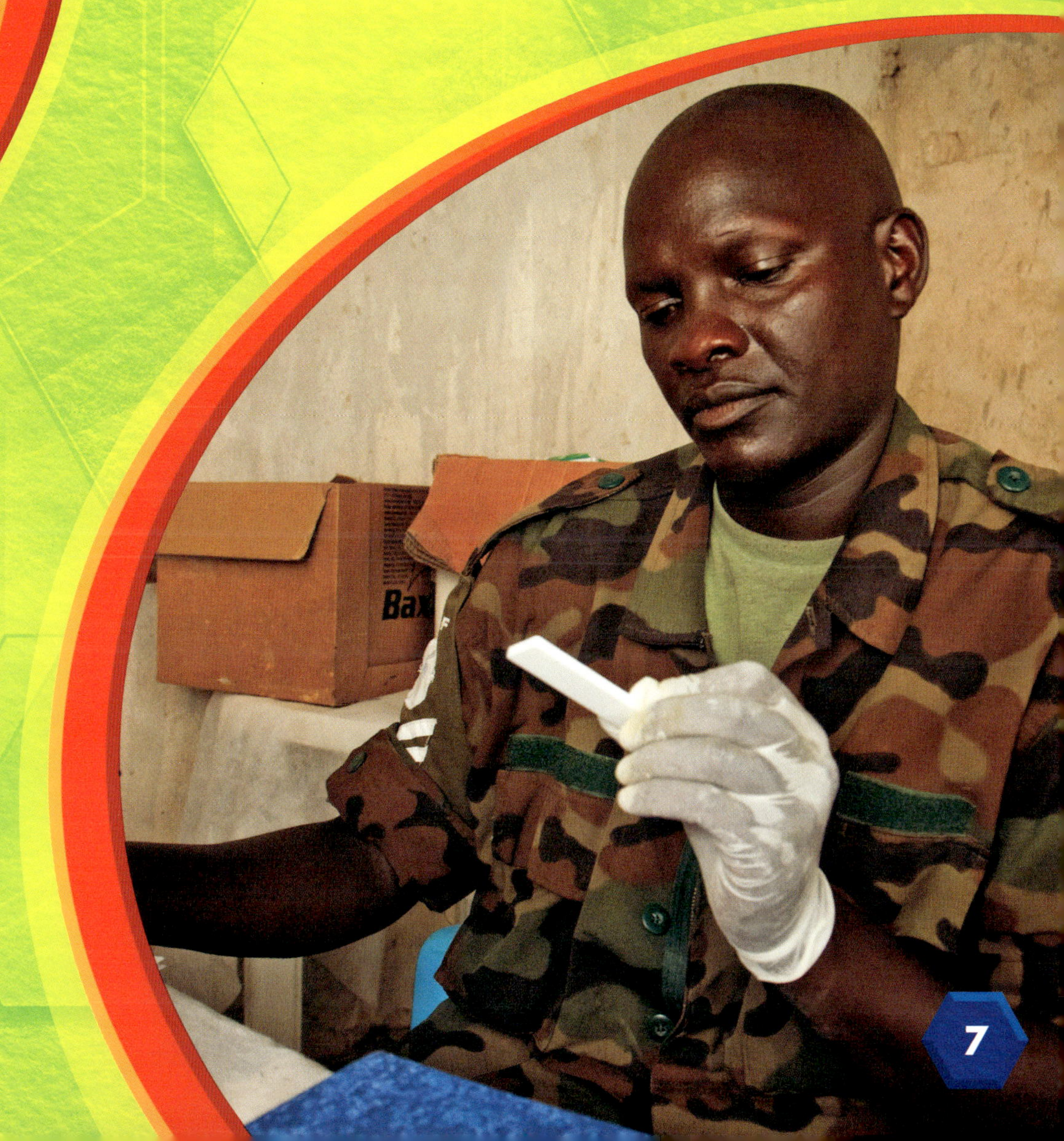

Some of these doctors meet with **patients**. They help people get better.

Famous Infectious Disease Specialist

Name	Anthony Fauci
Born	December 24, 1940
Birthplace	Brooklyn, New York
Schooling	College of the Holy Cross; Cornell University
Known For	helped respond to AIDS and COVID-19

Others track how sicknesses spread. They help stop sicknesses from hurting more people.

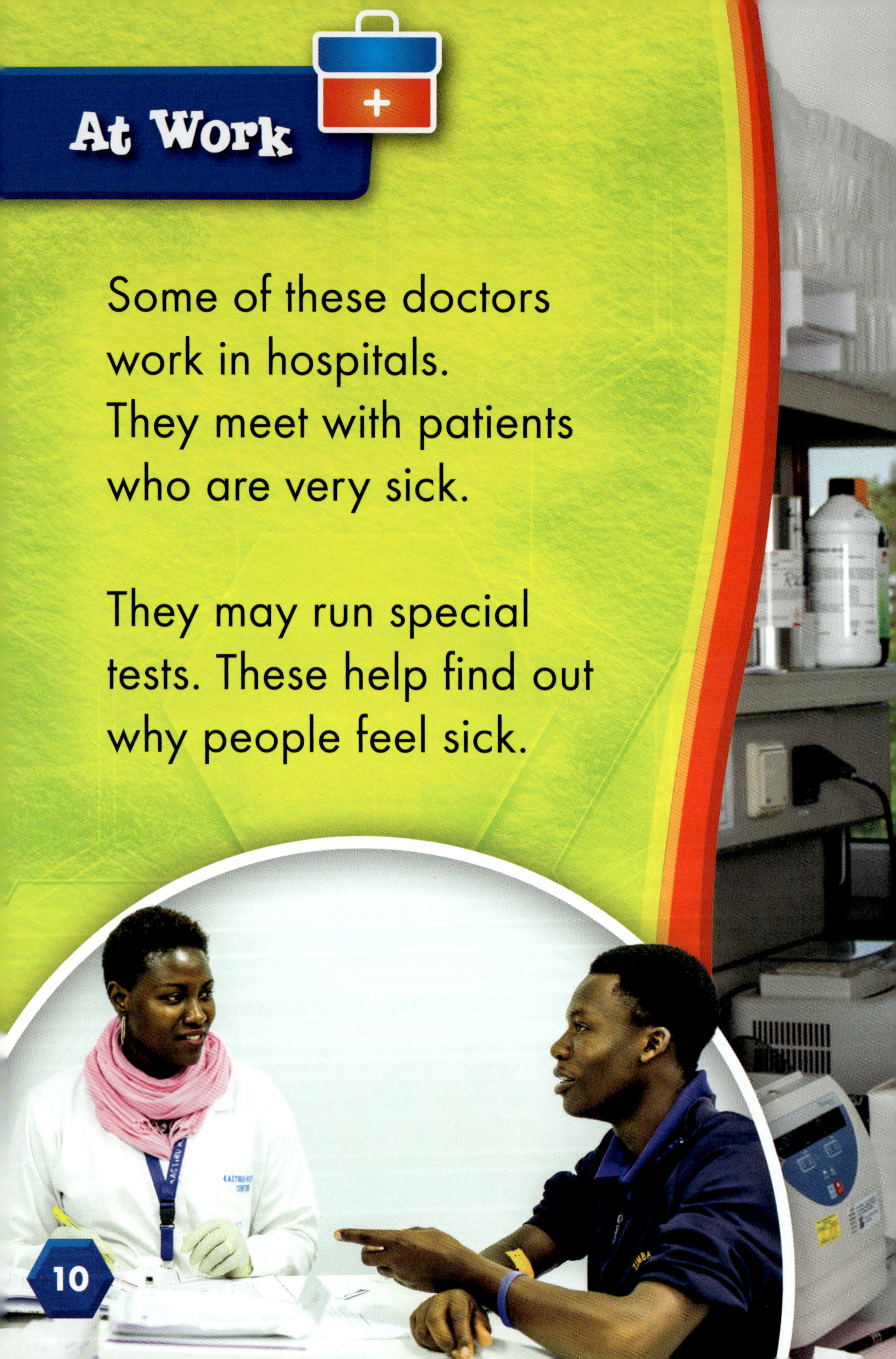

At Work

Some of these doctors work in hospitals. They meet with patients who are very sick.

They may run special tests. These help find out why people feel sick.

doctor running a test

They also help people who have a **chronic** sickness. These people are sick for a long time.

The doctors **prescribe** different medicines. They make plans if patients get worse.

Infectious Disease Specialists in Real Life

treatments for rare sicknesses

tracking new sicknesses

healthier people

Some of these doctors work in **labs**. They use **microscopes**. They find out what causes diseases. They track diseases with a computer.

Using STEM

Science — test ideas about how sicknesses spread

Technology — use computers to track sicknesses

Engineering — build hospitals to help stop sicknesses from spreading

Math — measure how fast sicknesses spread

They share their **research**.
This helps others be prepared!

Becoming an Infectious Disease Specialist

These doctors go to school for a long time. They go to college. They study **biology** and **chemistry**.

College usually takes four years. They study hard during this time.

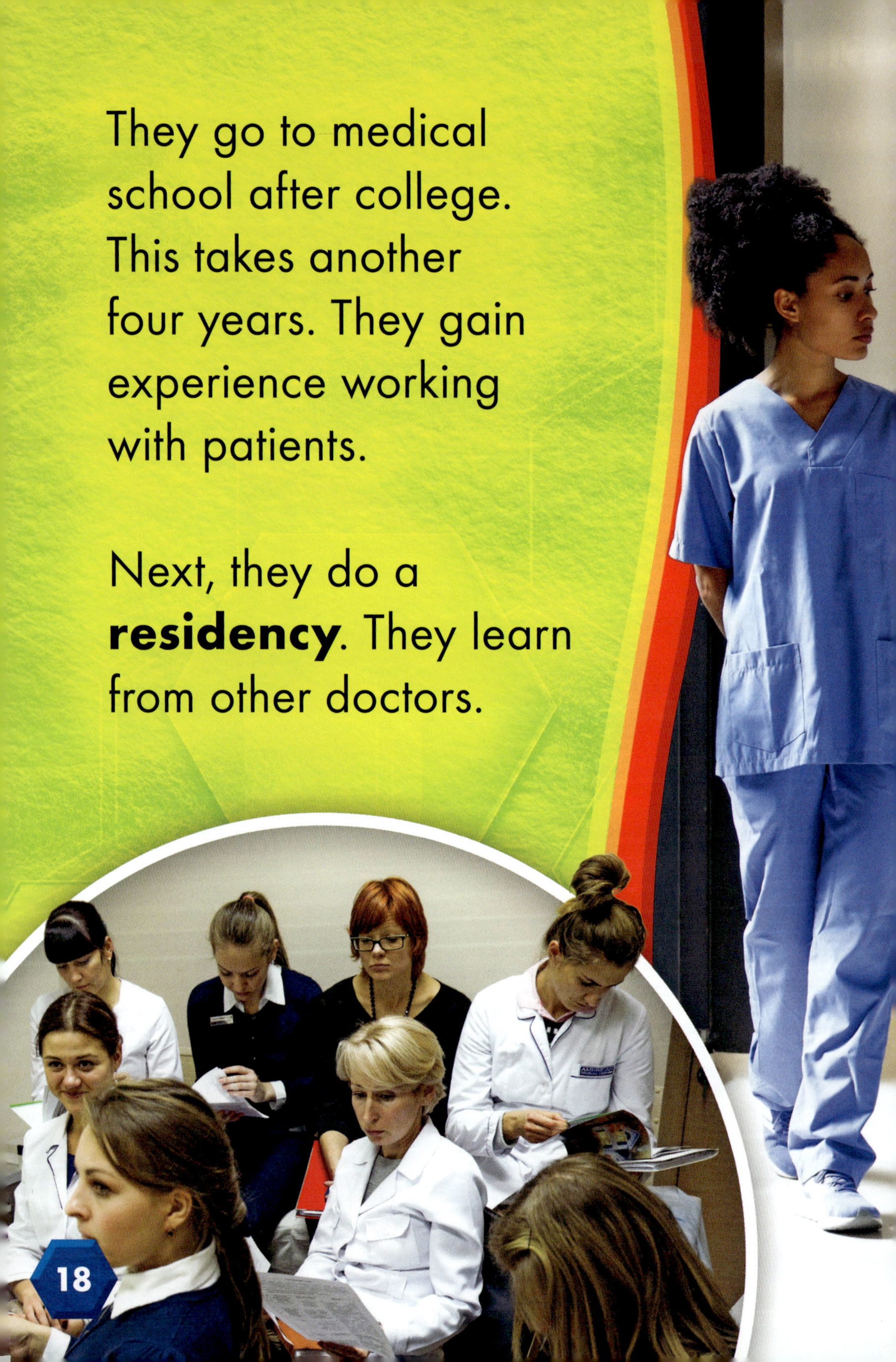

They go to medical school after college. This takes another four years. They gain experience working with patients.

Next, they do a **residency**. They learn from other doctors.

These doctors keep training in **fellowships**. They study diseases more closely. They learn more about what makes people sick.

How to Become an Infectious Disease Specialist

1. go to college
2. go to medical school
3. learn on the job in a residency

4. complete a fellowship

These special doctors help keep people healthy!

Glossary

biology—the scientific study of life

chemistry—a science that deals with substances and the changes they go through

chronic—lasting a long time or happening again and again

diseases—sicknesses

fellowships—periods of medical training after a residency is completed; fellowships give doctors more training in a certain area.

labs—buildings or rooms with special tools to do science experiments and tests

microscopes—tools used for looking at very small things

patients—people in need of medical care

prescribe—to order a certain medicine to be used to treat an illness

rare—not common

research—careful study to find new knowledge or information about something

residency—a time during which new doctors get work experience

To Learn More

AT THE LIBRARY

Bradley, Doug. *Doctor*. New York, N.Y.: PowerKids Press, 2023.

Moening, Kate. *Chemist*. Minneapolis, Minn.: Bellwether Media, 2022.

Redford, Ruth. *The Measles Files*. Rochester, Minn.: Mayo Clinic Press Kids, 2026.

ON THE WEB

FACTSURFER

Factsurfer.com gives you a safe, fun way to find more information.

1. Go to www.factsurfer.com.
2. Enter "infectious disease specialist" into the search box and click 🔍.
3. Select your book cover to see a list of related content.

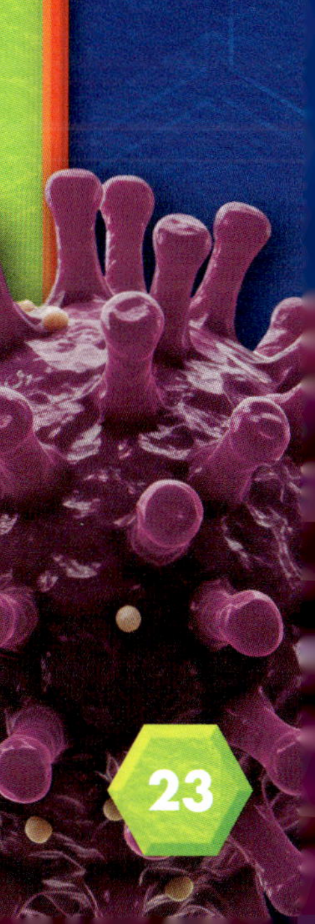

Index

The images in this book are reproduced through the courtesy of: FOTOGRIN, front cover (infectious disease specialist); gorodenkoff, front cover (lab); BillionPhotos.com, p. 3; tuachanwatthana, p. 4 (inset); 12521104, pp. 4-5; Boston Globe/ Contributor/ Getty Images, pp. 6-7 (top); AMISOM Public Information/ Wikipedia, p. 7; Christopher Michel/ Wikipedia, p. 8 (Fauci); eclipse_images/ Getty Images, pp. 8-9; Gilbert Sibomana/ Wikipedia, p. 10 (inset); U.S. Army TSAE by Volker Ramspott/ Wikipedia, pp. 10-11; DFID - UK Department for International Development/ Wikipedia, pp. 12-13; Navy Medicine, p. 13 (treatments); Sgt. Aaron Ellerman/ Wikipedia, p. 13 (tracking); Phil Roeder/ Wikipedia, p. 13 (healthier people); Abraham Gonzalez Fernandez/ Getty Images, pp. 14-15 (microscopes); Pablo Jarrín/ Wikipedia, p. 15 (inset); koldo studio, pp. 16-17 (top); SDI Productions, p. 17; B.globa/ Wikipedia, p. 18 (inset); Hispanolistic, pp. 18-19; Krakenimages.com, pp. 20-21 (infectious disease specialist); Milwaukee VA Medical Center/ Wikipedia, pp. 20-21 (top); James, p. 23.